MEXICO
A PICTURE BOOK TO REMEMBER HER BY

Designed by
DAVID GIBBON

Produced by
TED SMART

CRESCENT

INTRODUCTION

Mexico's colourful history begins with the Indians who inhabited the country some 2,000 or more years ago. Their knowledge of agriculture, astronomy, crafts and even political organisation far outreached that of their counterparts in the north. In turn, such brilliant civilisations as the Olmecs, Zapotecs, Mixtecs, Mayas, Toltecs and Aztecs all left their mark on the rich and fascinating Mexican landscape.

The most ancient civilisation was that of the Olmecs, whose indecipherable hieroglyphs were possibly the first writings in Mexico. They were also highly skilled in carving – particularly jade and basalt. Figurines, pendants, heads and altars in particular were their contribution to the country's archaeological wealth.

A culture reminiscent of the Olmecs emerged from the Valley of Oaxaca in the south, reflecting the combined achievements of the Zapotecs and Mixtecs. Their most famous site is at Monte Albán – a site developed over a period of 17 centuries. It is a huge area containing a wealth of pyramids, palaces, observatories and a large number of tombs which indicate the site's special character as a burial area or necropolis. With the decline of the Zapotecs the Mixtecs took over the, by then neglected, site and used it for the burial, in the tombs, of their lords and priests.

One of the most advanced races was the Maya, of which some two million still live in Mexico today, speaking one of the two dozen distinct Maya languages. The Maya's magnificent stone buildings and sculptures, a calendar as precise as our own, and progressive farming – without the use of metal tools – are features of their lifestyle. Their great understanding of mathematics and astronomy and their use of hieroglyphics are well-known but they also sacrificed human beings in their religious ceremonies, although to a lesser extent than the Aztecs. The breathtaking capital of Chichen Itza is renowned for its cenote or sacred well, 100 feet deep, into which sacrificial victims bearing jewels and offerings were thrown, especially in periods of drought.

The Maya way of life was soon superseded by that of the Toltecs, who came down from the High Plateau, and their capital, Tula, some 600 miles away, and overran the peaceful cities of the Yucatan. In addition, they founded their new capital at Chichen Itza. The Aztecs, in their turn, took over from the Toltecs and it was their civilization that was predominant in Mexico at the time of the Spanish Conquest in 1519. Agriculture formed the basis of their lives and in many other ways they adopted the culture of the people they had politically supplanted. They built massive pyramids, temples, palaces, excellent roads and were outstanding craftsmen, particularly in the making of jewellery. We know a great deal about their lives from the hieroglyphs and pictographs they left. One of the Maya's greatest achievements was in building the city of Tenochtitlán. Sited in the middle of a lagoon, it was a city of canals, bridges, shrines, palaces and some 60,000 houses. The Great Temple, which was reduced to rubble by the Conquistadores, now lies under the Zocalo, Mexico City's main square.

Under Montezuma I, the Aztecs extended their rule over much of Central and South Mexico. Their rule was very oppressive; so much so that Montezuma II, whose reign began in 1502, was only able to offer slight resistance to Hernando Cortés and his Spanish men-at-arms when they landed at Vera Cruz in 1519. So, with just a few hundred men Cortés took over the vast territory, which at that time included Texas, California and New Mexico, enslaved the people and destroyed the temples and other buildings. The Spaniards also imposed their Roman Catholic religion and their language and in time through intermarriage thus produced a new race of Mexicans.

For a time life was relatively tranquil but the rich minority were becoming progressively wealthier whereas the poor Indians were becoming steadily poorer. The Indians eventually rebelled and Spanish rule ended in Mexico in 1821. In 1824 a republic was set up from which, a few years later, Texas broke away and then, after the war of 1846–48, New Mexico and California were ceded to the U.S.A. and Mexico became greatly reduced in size.

After the three years of Civil War, Benito Juaréz, a Zapotec Indian, was elected President. He was a great reformer and worked towards a new nationalism. He is still regarded as a national hero and many monuments have been erected to his memory. One of the most decisive acts of his rule was the rejection of Emperor Maximilian, an Austrian Prince, who was sent, together with a number of French troops, by Napoleon III to re-establish monarchic rule in Mexico. The Republicans under Juaréz offered strong resistance and subsequently the French troops were withdrawn and Maximilian was executed by firing squad.

Another of the country's powerful leaders was Porfirio Diaz, who encouraged foreign investment, secured law and order, built railroads and aided the development of oilfields. He was also responsible for building great showplaces such as the Palace of Fine Arts in Mexico City. Despite this, he was in reality a dictator and he failed to meet the needs of the masses, many of whom were living in abject poverty. In 1910 another revolution took place and "land and liberty" was the familiar cry of the reformers Emiliano Zapata and Francisco "Pancho" Villa. It was this uprising that eventually led to Diaz fleeing to Europe.

Since the revolution there has been rapid industrialisation and great advances have been made in education and agriculture. The country is rich in minerals, and vast reserves of recently discovered oil and natural gas promise long-range economic stability. The capital, Mexico City, which has a population of some 12,000,000, is a sophisticated and cosmopolitan city which is very popular for conventions and international trade meetings.

A very important source of income comes from tourism. Mexico's palm-fringed beaches, luxury hotels and rich history are appreciated by an ever increasing number of visitors. Not only does tourism earn welcome foreign currency but it also creates much needed employment. The potential for this holiday paradise is vast, particularly along the Pacific coast, where Acapulco at the moment reigns supreme. With continuing political stability the future of Mexico and her people would appear to be an encouraging one.

Typical of the many colour washed houses to be found in Mexico is Puebla Street *left*.

Spectacular views over Mexico City
can be seen from the 44 storey Latin
American Tower *left and top right.*

The Column of Independence *above*
with its magnificent golden angel
overlooking the city reaches was
inaugurated in 1910 by General
Porfirio Diáz. At each corner of its
base are statues representing Law,
Justice, War and Peace. Also within
the Paseo de la Reforma is the lovely
fountain of Diana the Huntress
below.

The beautiful Palace of Fine Arts
centre right, situated on the east side
of Alameda Park, contains lecture
and exhibition halls and a theatre.

Another dazzling view of Mexico
City can be seen *right.*

Dominating the Zocalo in the heart of Mexico City is the Cathedral *above,* which was started in 1573 and finished only last century.

Designed to replace a smaller church built on the site of an Aztec temple in 1525, it combines various architectural styles; Ionic, Doric, Corinthian and Baroque, each reflecting the influence the numerous architects, kings, viceroys and bishops made on its design. Within the richly ornate interior *left, below and right* are several chapels and many priceless treasures.

The coloured towers of Goeritz *above* stand at the entrance to Satellite City and in contrast to this modern development is the beautiful Chapultepec Park *above left* with its large lakes and extensive woodland.

One of Mexico City's showpiece - stadiums is the Aztec *above right,* which provides room for over 100,000 spectators, whilst *below right* can be seen the University Stadium which was the site of the 1968 Olympic Games. University Village is pictured *bottom left.*

Bullfighting is a popular sport throughout Mexico and the city's impressive bullring and stadium is seen *centre right.*

Mexico City's road systems provide numerous interesting aerial views, *far right, centre left and below.* Wide straight avenues and complicated intersections keep the traffic running smoothly.

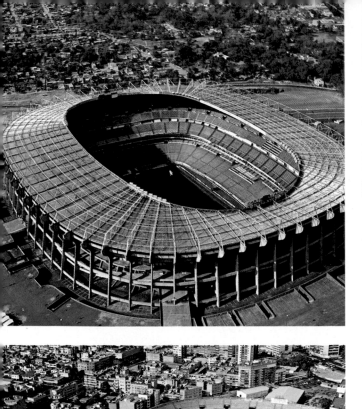

One of the most important and lively markets in Mexico City is held in La Merced *top left;* and *above* can be seen one of the elaborate walls of the library in University City.

The vast esplanade of the Plaza of the Three Cultures *left* contains some of the archaeological remains of the Aztec world, and *below left* is another splendid view of the Palace of Fine Arts.

Alameda Park *top right* is one of the most beautiful in the city and *below right* is a dazzling night view of the Independence Monument.

The House of Tiles at Sanborns *below,* now a popular restaurant, is one of the city's most famous landmarks with its distinctive blue and white facade.

One of the most renowned sights of Mexico City is the floating gardens of Zochimilco *top left and right*. The gardens are criss-crossed by canals lined with poplar trees – and colourful gondolas, known as trajineras, may be hired to explore the waterways.

Mexico's best known artist, Diego Rivera, used Alameda Park as a setting for some of his paintings and *left* can be seen the mouthwatering fruits which are sold in the park, whilst *above* the colourful balloons are yet another attraction.

Art Exhibitions in the Jardin Des Arts *below left* are also a popular Sunday feature and the gaily woven rugs *below* make wonderful souvenirs.

A wide variety of handicrafts can be haggled for in Mexico City's many markets *above and left*. Carved wooden masks, ornaments, silver plate and goblets and even old horse shoes are amongst the many items which are on sale.

Bullfighting *right* is an important spectator sport throughout Mexico, arousing the strongest of passions and bravery is usually shown on both sides of the bright red cape.

During the formal season which commences on December 1st and lasts for three or four months, the top matadors compete against bulls which can weigh as much as 1,000 pounds.

Less experienced matadors, known as novilleros, fight smaller bulls during the remainder of the year.

Singing and dancing is popular as a form of relaxation and entertainment throughout Mexico. Mexicans like to enjoy themselves and there are more than 120 fêtes and festivals in the course of a year in towns and villages all over the country.

At Puerto Vallarta in Baja California, a picturesque and popular holiday resort, dancers in exotic coloured costumes, together with their accomplished accompanists, put on a spectacular display *these pages and overleaf*, where beautiful Mexican senoritas with billowing dresses, twist and whirl to the throbbing music.

Taxco, south of Mexico City, is a picturesque town clinging to a steep hillside. Narrow, twisting, cobbled streets and red-roofed houses are dominated by the pink stone of the Baroque church of San Prisca *above and top right*, reputed to be the most perfect example of ecclesiastical art ever produced during the entire 300-year Colonial period.

Ranching *below left* is important in the area and travelling by horseback *top left*, a favourite method of transport.

Fruit and vegetables piled high on a market stall create a colourful scene *right*, whilst *below* the market traders sit in the welcome shade of the nearby buildings.

An example of the cracked dry land completely dehydrated by the scorching sun can be seen *centre left*.

Near the famous ceramics city of Puebla is the magnificent Church of San Francisco Acatepec *above and left*, a masterpiece of Baroque art and architecture covered with colourful 'azulejos' which glint like porcelain in the sunshine.

The exquisite tiled columns *far left* and heavily gilded interior *right* are a truly majestic sight, enjoyed by all who visit this beautiful church.

Morelia, originally known as Valladolid,
was founded in 1541 and is one of
Mexico's most delightful cities. One of
its many attractive buildings is the
Cathedral *left and above*, which was
started in 1660 and completed in 1744.

Twenty-five miles north-east of Mexico
City is the vast, majestic archaeological
site of Teotihuacan, named the 'City of
the Gods' by the Aztecs, whose largest
and oldest monument, the Pyramid of
the Sun *below and right*, was
constructed about 100 B.C.

After the defeat of the Aztecs their shrines and temples were replaced by Catholic Churches. The town of Cholula is said to have had 365 churches, one for each day of the year.

On the outskirts of the town stands the richly embellished Church of Santa Maria Tonantzintla *these pages*, encompassing intricately carved towers and heavily ornamented cupolas.

San Miguel de Allende *above* is a fine
Colonial town with picturesque streets
and lovely courtyard gardens, some of
which can be seen on these pages.

Metal working in tin, iron, brass, gold
and silver is an important occupation
and it was here that Ignacio Allende, a
leader in Mexico's early struggle for
Independence, was born.

One of the largest lakes in Mexico is the island-dotted Lake Patzcuaro, where the famed butterfly fishermen *above* ply the blue waters with their graceful, dipping nets.

Life in the Indian town of Patzcuaro has barely changed since Colonial days and the people spend most of their time fishing on the lake, or at home producing a variety of handicrafts, including excellent pottery and copperware as shown *opposite*.

Tula was the great city of the warrior Toltecs. The terraced pyramid *far left,* a wonderful legacy left by these accomplished builders, is surmounted by huge Atlantes *left,* which provide support for the roof of the temple above the pyramid.

The charming town of Puerto Vallarta retains much of its tranquillity in its lovely old buildings and cobbled streets, where the mellow Guadeloupe Church in the main square can be seen *right*. This prosperous holiday resort with magnificent hotels and an international airport, draws many visitors who come to enjoy its extensive facilities and sympathetic climate.

Guadalajara is the second city of Mexico and a city of fine Colonial character. The grand cathedral *left and below left* was begun in 1561 and is surrounded by four impressive plazas.

A relaxing mode of transport in Guadalajara is the picturesque horse-drawn carriage *above*.

The hotels within the area are truly superb *below*, with many impressive features to pamper and cosset the discerning guest.

Puerto Vallarta *bottom left* has many wide, white, sandy beaches *right*, all lapped by a gentle blue sea.

The lovely Mismaloya Beach *above*, discovered by Hollywood several years ago, was used as the location for the shooting of the film, 'Night of the Iguana'.

The attractive beach *left* is used by the residents of the Garza Blanca Hotel, and *below* can be seen another fine hotel, the 'Holiday Inn'.

The spectacular cliff formation near Acapulco, known as La Quebrada, is world famous for the daredevil performances of its divers *right*. The divers require a great deal of skill, and accurate judgement is crucial in order to slip safely between the narrow crevice of the rocks.

At the base of La Quebrada is an observation platform or belvedere as it is known *above, left and far left*, from where visitors can watch the exciting feats of the divers.

Acapulco, the largest and most popular of Mexico's resorts, still manages to retain its natural beauty and tranquil atmosphere.

There are approximately 38 beautiful beaches, and Hornos Beach *top left, bottom left and below* is known as the 'Afternoon Beach', because of the late afternoon sunshine which attracts many Mexican families who can laze under the shade of pretty thatched umbrellas. A young girl *above* sells tortoises and armadillos on the beach.

Wonderful Condesa Beach *centre left and right* is especially popular with young people.

Overleaf. The day-time view of Acapulco's skyline *right* is transformed into a dazzling vista by night *left*.

Life is never dull in Acapulco for a wide variety of water sports, tennis, golf and even parachute jumping *above* can be enjoyed in this holiday paradise.

The splendid waterfront *above and below right* provides good moorings for boats of every shape and size, whilst pretty, coloured sailing vessels can be seen on Revolcadero Beach *above left*.

Caleta Beach, encircling a small tropical bay *below, bottom and below left*, is enjoyed by many local people and has a gay Mexican air.

Another stunning night view of Acapulco Bay is shown *overleaf*.

Acapulco's luxurious hotels, with their extensive facilities, ensure a delightful stay for visitors to this exotic holiday centre.

The Acapulco Princess Hotel *opposite page* is built in a unique pyramid design and boasts several outstanding pools, some of which contain fabulous cascading falls such as the one shown *below*.

The Hotel Torre Playasol *above* is a further example of the supreme quality offered by the hotels within the area and *left* can be seen the fantastic fish-shaped pool which is a particular feature of this hotel.

The Yucatan Peninsula is one of the most fascinating regions in the whole of Mexico, where most of the Maya sites are located. Merida, the capital of the Yucatan State, is known as the 'white city' and was founded in 1542, upon the site of an ancient Maya town, by Francisco de Montejo. Pretty pastel-coloured houses with fragrant flowers adorning their patios, can be seen throughout the city and horse-drawn carriages lend enchantment, especially when seen by night.

One of the loveliest buildings in the city is the arcaded Municipal Palace, whether seen by day *above right*, or by night *near left*.

Overlooking the Oxaca Valley is the vast and overwhelming archaeological site of Monte Alban *left and below left.* Ruined temples, remains of pyramids, tombs, underground passages and an ancient ballcourt are the silent reminders of a once thriving community which owed its being to the Zapotecs.

A few miles away lies Mitla *this page,* which with its magnificent palaces was the centre of the Mixtec world. Here are to be seen many splendid structures each faced with geometrically designed mosaics whose patterns combine in imagery of the 'Plumed Serpent'.

The splendour of the ancient city of
Uxmal owes much to the symmetry
achieved by the Maya tribesmen and it
is considered to be the most successful
achievement of the Maya civilisation.
Dominating the site is the Temple of the
Magician *left*, an oval pyramid which is
also known as the Pyramid of the
Soothsayer.

To the west lies the Nunnery
Quadrangle *below left*, reminiscent of
the cloistered quarters of a convent and
richly embellished at roof level with a
frieze of stone mosaics.

The most visited of all ancient Maya
cities is Chichén Itzá which has been
extensively restored on the northern
side of the site.

The Temple of the Warriors *right and
below* is decorated with wall-carvings
and Toltec Warriors. The serpent-
shaped columns are typical of those
found in the temple.

Another splendid view can be seen *above* of the Temple of the Warriors, also known as the Temple of a Thousand Columns.

The Caracol or Observatory *centre right*, at Chichén Itzá, derives its name from the spiral staircase inside the structure which is said to curl like the shell of a snail. This important building has apertures in the sides of its walls which, on certain dates would align with the stars and so enable the priests to adjust the Maya calendar.

The Castillo *top right*, a massive pyramid towering 75 feet high, was used as a fortress by the Spanish. One of the incredible pyramid stairways can be seen *right*.

Sixty-five miles south of Merida is the archaeological site of Kabah *left*, from where Maya religious processions once proceeded along the white road to Uxmal.

Cancun Island is one of the newest holiday resorts in the Mexican Caribbean. Although not technically an island, the turquoise waters that almost surround it are clear and inviting and ideal for snorkelling and skin-diving. The tempting, white, sandy beaches and secluded lagoons, together with the lush tropical vegetation, make it an ideal spot for sunworshippers, whilst the extensive sporting facilities are perfect for the more energetic.

Tulum *centre left, below left and below,* once a Maya fortress city and one of many along the Caribbean coast, was among the last bulwarks of the Maya culture. One of its more unusual features is the plan of the city centre, which was laid out in straight, building lined streets. This is in direct contrast to those of other Maya cities where the buildings tended to be grouped around central plazas.

The main building, El Castillo *left,* looks out over the cliffs and is a pyramidal structure crowned by a two-roomed temple.

Tranquil waters of Xel-Ha Lagoon *below* cover the submerged ruins of the site of a Maya city and make scuba-diving an even more exciting pastime.

Close by is Akumal *right,* a secluded seaside resort with perfect palm-fringed beaches and an excellent base for visitors who wish to explore Tulum.

The Spanish Conquistadores named the Isla Mujeres, which translated means 'island of women', after the numerous terracotta figurines they found among the Maya ruins when they discovered the island. This tiny island, surrounded by coral gardens and reefs, offers an abundance of sun and sea, fishing and diving, in a beautiful, unspoilt setting.

Billowing clouds in a pink and mauve sky wash over the island at sunset *overleaf.*

First published in Great Britain 1978 by Colour Library International Ltd.
© Illustrations: Colour Library International Ltd. Colour separations by La Cromolito, Milan, Italy.
Display and text filmsetting by Focus Photoset, London, England.
Printed and bound by L.E.G.O. Vicenza, Italy.
Published by Crescent Books, a division of Crown Publishers Inc.
All rights reserved.
Library of Congress Catalogue Card No. 78-60454
CRESCENT 1978